WORLD WAR II

The Full Story

Behind the Lines

Published by Brown Bear Books Ltd
4877 N. Circulo Bujia
Tucson, AZ 85718
USA

and

First Floor
9-17 St. Albans Place
London N1 0NX

ISBN: 978-1-78121-234-9

Library of Congress Cataloging-in-Publication
Data available upon request

Managing Editor: Tim Cooke
Designer: Lynne Lennon
Picture Manager: Sophie Mortimer
Editorial Director: Lindsey Lowe
Design Manager: Keith Davis
Children's Publisher: Anne O'Daly
Production Director: Alastair Gourlay

Manufactured in the United States of America

CPSIA compliance information: Batch# AG/5566

CONTENTS

INTRODUCTION

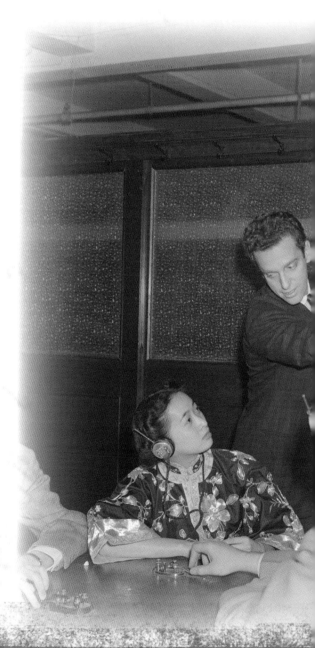

Behind the front lines of World War II (1939–1945), both the Allies and the Axis powers sought ways to gain any advantage they could over the enemy. These efforts meant that virtually everyone in combatant countries was eventually directly involved in the war in one way or another.

War at Sea and in the Air

Once the Germans had conquered most of mainland Europe, they turned their attention to Britain. When they were defeated in the Battle of Britain in 1940, they instead set out to use U-boats (submarines) to prevent the British receiving supplies from North America. Eventually that would force Britain into surrendering in order to avoid starvation. The Battle of the Atlantic is the name given to the long struggle by the Allies to keep the sea lanes open. The battle was the longest of the war—it lasted over five years, and cost thousands of lives. The Allies, meanwhile, planned to bomb

→ U.S. students learn to decipher Japanese codes at an Aeronautical Radio School in 1943.

➜ A victorious German U-boat (submarine) crew celebrate as they return to port from the Atlantic Ocean.

Germany into surrender with a massive air campaign. German cities were destroyed and German civilians killed in raids that often involved more than 1,000 bombers at a time.

Technology at War

The sea and air wars, like all aspects of the war, reflected new technology. World War II marked one of the most intense periods of technological development in history, as scientists on both sides tried to improve weaponry, transportation, communications, and medical care. They also put huge efforts into encoding messages for security—and on breaking the codes of the enemy. That quest to gain intelligence about the enemy was closely allied to the use of espionage, or spies, to gather information.

WAR IN THE ATLANTIC

Britain relied on supplies from overseas, especially from the United States. Keeping the sea lanes open was essential if Britain was to survive.

ritish prime minister Winston Churchill once wrote "The only thing that ever really frightened me during the war was the U-boat peril." U-boats were German submarines (*Underseeboote*, or "undersea-boats") that preyed on transatlantic shipping. If Germany gained control of the Atlantic, it could starve Britain into surrender and gain control of all of Europe.

The Longest Battle Begins

When Britain entered World War II in 1939, the Royal Navy was the largest navy in the world. It had far more warships than the German navy, the *Kriegsmarine*. The Germans knew they could not take on the British fleet in battle.

→ Two German U-boats undergo training exercises in the Baltic Sea.

← Crewmen on a German cruiser watch an Allied merchant ship sink after they have attacked it.

Instead, the Kriegsmarine commander, Grand Admiral Erich Raeder, decided to sink merchant vessels carrying supplies to Britain. Many of the vessels came from North America. Raeder deployed warships far out in the Atlantic to intercept them, while U-boats patrolled the British coast. The Germans also laid mines in Britain's coastal waters and used long-range maritime aircraft to search for targets.

POCKET BATTLESHIPS

Introduced into service by Germany in the 1930s, pocket battleships were fast, heavily armed commerce raiders that could overtake and sink merchant ships, outgun enemy cruisers, and outrun full-size battleships. The three German pocket battleships were initially highly effective, but the Allies then improved their tactics, which removed the German advantage.

KEY WEAPONS

U-BOATS

Early in the war, U-boats usually hunted alone. They only attacked on the surface, using their deck guns. As more U-boats were built, they adopted a tactic of attacking a convoy in a "wolf pack" of 15 or 20 vessels. They attacked together at night from all directions. Later in the war, faster Allied escort ships and increased naval air power ended the wolf pack threat.

The Convoy System

Hours after Britain declared war on Germany on September 3, 1939, the *U-30* sank the British passenger liner *Athenia* with the loss of more than 110 civilians. Britain's response was to adopt a convoy system in which warships escorted groups of merchant ships to protect them from attack. The system had first been used in World War I (1914–1918). Aircraft carriers formed patrol groups to hunt for U-boats. The British, however, did not have enough smaller ships, which were more effective at hunting U-boats.

The German U-boats scored a number of victories, including penetrating Scapa Flow, the Royal Navy's main base in the

⬇ A U-boat close to the English coast in 1940. They spent time on the surface when travelling longer distances.

Orkney Islands, north of Scotland. Meanwhile, in the South Atlantic and southern Indian Ocean, German warships sank 11 merchant ships between September and December 1939. The British chased the German pocket battleship, *Graf Spee*, to the River Plate in neutral Uruguay. Trapped, its captain deliberately sank his ship and killed himself.

By the end of 1939, the British were holding their own in the North Atlantic. Allied losses stood at 114 ships sunk by U-boats and around 80 by mines, but these losses were manageable. A year later, however, the British seemed to be losing the Battle of the Atlantic.

The Kriegsmarine Progresses

Following the surrender of Norway and France in June 1940, Germany gained an advantage. It now had bases on the Atlantic that increased the reach of its U-boats and made it easier for German long-range aircraft to locate targets. The British had meanwhile diverted ships from the Atlantic to combat Adolf Hitler's planned invasion of England. Royal Navy ships now accompanied convoys only up to 200 miles (320 km) west of Ireland. The U-boats, however, could hunt up to 700 miles (1,120 km) out in the Atlantic. This meant they could attack virtually unopposed.

↑ The German battleship *Bismarck* fires shells during the Battle of the Denmark Strait in May 1941.

EYEWITNESS ACCOUNT

❝You could see the torpedo's trail as it knifed through the water toward the helpless *Patroclus*. A massive explosion rocked the ship when the torpedo struck and knocked us off our feet. The *Patroclus* began to list, but the U-boat continued to fire more torpedoes into the doomed ship.❞

George Clarke
Sailor on HMS *Patroclus*, sunk in November 1940

→ Survivors from a sinking Allied merchant ship row toward a U-boat to be taken prisoner.

The "Happy Time"

Although no more than sixteen U-boats operated in the North Atlantic at any time, they sank 3 million tons (2.7 million metric tons) of shipping in the second half of 1940. German submariners called this the "Happy Time." By December 1940, the British had lost 20 percent of their prewar merchant fleet and could not build replacements fast enough. Nor could they sink the U-boats. By the end of 1940 only six had been sunk by the Royal Navy.

In 1941, Germany was producing twenty U-boats each month, and the German Atlantic operation grew quickly.

Operations were extended to the central and western Atlantic. Admiral Karl Dönitz, commander of the force, developed a new tactic. When a U-boat spotted a convoy, it radioed its position to others in the area. Fifteen or twenty U-boats would converge on the convoy in a "wolf pack" and attack. By the end of 1941, submarines had sunk some 432 Allied ships—although this was fewer than the sinkings in 1940.

The Surface War

Germany's surface fleet had mixed fortunes. In four-months of 1940, the pocket battleship *Admiral Scheer* had destroyed 17 Allied vessels. In March 1941, the surface raiders *Scharnhorst* and *Gneisenau* sank 16 merchant ships in two days. They were later bombed by the RAF while in dry dock in Germany and were effectively put out of action.

Germany's most powerful battleship was the *Bismarck*. In May 1941, during the Battle of the Denmark Strait, it sank

U.S. SINKINGS

Even before the United States entered the war in December 1941, its merchant and naval ships were active in the Atlantic. From September 1941, warships began to protect convoys. The destroyer USS *Kearny* was damaged by a U-boat in October, and on October 31 another destroyer, USS *Reuben James*, was sunk. The attacks hardened U.S. feeling against Germany.

Britain's flagship battlecruiser HMS *Hood* and badly damaged HMS *Prince of Wales*. The British sent four battleships, two battle cruisers, two aircraft carriers, twelve cruisers and several destroyers to track down *Bismarck*. It was found and sunk on May 26, 1941. Only 110 of its 2,200 crew survived.

In the months that followed the sinking of *Bismarck*, British vessels sank or captured many of the supply vessels that supported Germany's warships. The Allies were also learning how to remove the

← This picture shows the cramped conditions in the forward torpedo room of a German U-boat.

→ A crewman struggles across the deck as his U-boat begins to sink after an Allied attack.

threat of sea mines. Their equipment had improved: they now had radar that could detect targets on the surface. The British had also developed a small escort carrier. This type of ship could carry six fighter planes, which could spot U-boats and fight off German long-range reconnaissance aircraft.

During the last three months of 1941, Allied shipping losses in the Atlantic fell dramatically as antisubmarine operations improved and Hitler ordered 25 U-boats to be diverted to the Mediterranean. But it was the involvement of the United States that gave Britain hope. In March 1941, Congress passed the Lend-Lease

SAINT-NAZAIRE RAID

In early 1942, the British planned to destroy the dry dock at Saint-Nazaire, France, to stop the German battleship *Tirpitz* operating in the Atlantic. The plan was to ram the dock gate using an old destroyer packed with explosives armed with delay fuses. Meanwhile, commandos would demolish shore installations. The raid went ahead early on March 28, but the evacuation of the commandos went wrong. Only 228 of the 621 raiders returned to Britain. Later that morning, the destroyer blew up, killing 360 Germans and wrecking the dock.

Act, which authorized President Roosevelt to "lend" equipment to the Allies (they were to pay when the war was over). The United States sent troops to Iceland to take over bases used by the British. Although not yet at war, U.S. warships escorted Allied convoys west of Greenland, meaning Britain's warships could be released from escort duties.

Battle of the Atlantic 1942–1945

Until the end of 1941, the United States was technically neutral. After the Japanese bombing of Pearl Harbor on

> **"**There is a frightful crack, just as if the boat has been struck by a gigantic hammer. Electric bulbs and glasses fly about, leaving fragments everywhere. Reports from all stations show, thank God, that there are no leaks—just the main fuses blown. The damage is made good.**"**
>
> Heinz Schaefer recalls being depth-charged on *U-977*, 1942

↓ A mine scores a direct hit on a U-boat. U-boats on the surface were also vulnerable to air attack.

⬆ The German battle cruiser *Scharnhorst* was immensely fast and could sail at a top speed of 38 mph (61 kmh).

December 7, it entered the war. Admiral Dönitz diverted much of his U-boat force from the central Atlantic to patrol off the East Coast of the United States. With the coastal lights silhouetting targets, the U-boats successfully sank a number of ships until U.S. authorities enforced a "dim-out" lights policy. Between January and June 1942, U-boats sank 327 U.S. ships between Maine and the Caribbean. Further attacks on Atlantic convoys resulted in between six and eight million tons of Allied shipping losses in 1942. The U-boat commanders called this their second "Happy Time."

Defeating the U-Boats

By mid-1942, however, the economic might of the United States was turning the battle in the Atlantic. U.S. shipyards geared up to produce "Liberty ships," which were prefabricated merchant vessels built to a standard template in under three months each. More merchant ships were being produced than the U-boats could destroy.

Dönitz switched his U-boats to the so-called Atlantic air gap— a stretch of sea that lay beyond the range of Allied land-based aircraft. By March 1943, there were 240 U-boats in the air gap.

Sinkings of merchant vessels rose again as German tactics became more effective. The Germans also changed their naval codes, which defeated Allied decoders.

But with rapid developments in Allied antisubmarine tactics and technology, the numbers of U-boats being sunk soon began to increase in turn. New radar technology in aircraft allowed crews to precisely locate a submarine on the ocean surface. In May 1943, the development of Very Long Range (VLR) Liberator aircraft, with a flying range of over 3,000

CONVOY PQ17

The destruction of PQ17 was the lowest point in the operation to supply Russia via the Arctic. The convoy came under air attack in July 1942. When reports suggested a large surface force was about to attack, Admiral Sir Dudley Pound ordered the ships of the convoy to scatter. In fact, that left them vulnerable to U-boats and German bombers, which sank 26 ships of the convoy.

miles (4,800 km) closed the mid-Atlantic air gap. The same month, Allied code-breakers broke the new German naval codes. Such measures combined with introduction of an antisubmarine torpedo that guided itself to its target. In May 1943, the Allies sank 47 U-boats.

With unsustainable losses, Dönitz withdrew his U-boat fleet to France. The following year, after the Allied invasion of France in June 1944, the Allies seized many submarine stations along the French coast. New submarine

← Survivors from the U.S. steamer *Carlton*, one of the ships in Convoy PQ17.

← Crews on Arctic
convoys faced
freezing conditions
in addition to enemy
attacks. They wore
numerous layers of
thick clothing.

war effort. The fist convoy sailed for Russia on August 21, 1941, Each convoy was given a number and two letters: PQ indicated that the convoy was outbound and QP designated homeward convoys.

Action in the Arctic

With air temperatures often below zero, ships on the Arctic convoys often iced up. There were frequent storms. In spring 1942, the German land campaign against Russia stopped. The Germans turned their attention to Russia's North Atlantic supply lifeline, launching all available resources—U-boats, bombers, fast torpedo boats, and large warships (such as the *Tirpitz*, *Admiral Hipper*, and *Lützow*)—against the Arctic convoys.

While the warships made a limited impact on the convoys, the U-boats and bomber aircraft inflicted heavy losses. In July 1942, 26 out of 37 Allied ships were sunk. As a result, the British improved

technology arrived too late to be of use and in May 1945, the Kriegsmarine surrendered with the rest of the German forces. The U-boat crews had suffered the highest percentage of deaths of any part of the German military.

The Arctic War

From August 1941, the Atlantic War was accompanied by another bitter naval conflict. Allied Arctic convoys delivered huge quantities of U.S. and British goods to the Soviet Union, sailing from Britain and Iceland via the Barents Sea. The convoys delivered more than 22 percent of the Land-Lease supplies sent to the Soviet Union and were vital to the Soviet

their escort tactics. In December 1942, the two sides clashed when the Germans attacked convoy JW51B (JW was the new code for outbound journeys). British escort vessels sank a German destroyer and damaged others. The German vessels returned to port to escape. A furious Hitler forced the commander of the Kriegsmarine, Grand Admiral Erich Raeder, to resign. Dönitz replaced him, but also kept command of the U-boats.

IN THE ARCTIC

The biggest problem for the crews on the Arctic convoys was the cold. Temperatures fell to as low as -76°F (-60°C). Frostbite was common and eyelashes were frozen together. Crews had to use axes and steam hoses to break ice off the decks. They wore numerous layers of thick, heavy clothing. Violent storms created waves 100 feet (32 m) high, causing seasickness.

The Tide Turns

Worse was to come. The pride of the German navy, *Tirpitz*, was put out of action by British midget submarines in September 1943. The *Scharnhost* was sunk on December 26, 1943. While under repair in Norway in November 1944, *Tirpitz* was destroyed by RAF bombers. By the end of 1944, the Allies had won the battle of the Arctic convoys. By February 1945, more than one U-boat was destroyed for every ship the Germans sank. The convoys had maintained the lifelines of the Allied war effort in Europe.

← The German battleship *Tirpitz* was a constant threat to Allied convoys.

WAR IN THE AIR

As early as 1940, the Germans launched a bombing campaign against Britain. The Allies responded with an air campaign of their own.

The German Luftwaffe began the Blitz, a bombing campaign against British cities, in September 1940. For nearly 40 weeks, German bombers made nighttime raids against British cities, particularly London. During the summer of 1941, Britain's Royal Air Force (RAF) managed to turn the tide of the German air attack. While Hitler had targeted British cities, however, Britain had not yet attacked German cities.

British Attacks

In late 1939, the RAF had made small daytime raids against German military targets, but heavy losses forced them to switch to nighttime raids. During 1940, the RAF concentrated its attacks on German factories that produced oil from coal in an effort to cripple the German war economy. But the RAF's equipment was not accurate enough to allow planes

← Cologne Cathedral stands amid ruins after the RAF's 1,000-bomber raid on May 30, 1942.

to navigate at night or to bomb specific targets, and German factories were protected by a network of fighters and antiaircraft guns directed by radar.

To counter this, in fall 1941 Bomber Command—one section of the RAF—switched from pinpoint attacks on specific targets to "area bombing." This meant British bombers now targeted not just factories but large areas surrounding them. A controversial strategy, area bombing aimed to weaken German civilian morale as well as destroying industry, transportation networks, power

⬇ American P-51 Mustang fighter aircraft take part in a daylight raid against Germany.

❝The raging fires in a high wind caused terrific damage and the grievous loss of human life. The fiery wind tore the roofs from the houses, uprooted large trees and flung them into the air like blazing torches. The inhabitants took refuge in the air-raid shelters, in which later they were burned to death or suffocated.❞

Wilhelm Johnen
on the Allied bombing of Hamburg, August 1943

← Arthur Harris (center, with glasses) and his staff plan a bombing raid.

and water services, and the homes of German workers. Bombing civilian targets is against international law and many British politicians and military leaders opposed area bombing. But after the German bombings of Coventry and London in 1940 during the Blitz, opinion in Britain gradually changed.

Arthur "Bomber" Harris

On February 22, 1942, Bomber Command received a boost with the arrival of its new commander-in-chief, Arthur "Bomber" Harris. Harris was aggressive and single-minded and immediately set about transforming Bomber Command.

He ordered the manufacture of thousands of heavy bombers, introduced electronic equipment to combat German radar defenses, and developed new tactics to attack specific targets with large numbers of bombers. Harris first used area bombing against the German city of Lübeck on the night of March 28, 1942, when some 234 aircraft destroyed 200 acres (81 ha) of the city. An attack on the port of Rostock in April 1942 was just as destructive. Hitler responded with the so-called Baedeker Raids. They were named for a series of German travel guides, because they targeted historic places in Britain that were popular with tourists, such as Exeter, Bath, and York.

KEY EVENTS

DAMBUSTERS RAID

One of the most daring RAF raids on Germany was a strike on dams near the Ruhr industrial region on May 16, 1943. The attack used a bomb designed to "bounce" along the water then explode as it sank to the base of the dam. The bombers had to fly low and straight—eight of the nineteen aircraft were lost. Two dams were ruptured, causing serious flooding and disrupting transportation links.

↓ Water gushes through the broken Möhne dam after the Dambusters Raid.

The success of the attacks on Lübeck and Rostock led Harris to plan for a huge air raid on the German city of Cologne. On May 30, 1942, some 1,087 bombers arrived over the city within 90 minutes of each other, maximizing the psychological effect on the civilians below and stretching German defenses. Only 41 bombers were lost but the raid killed 469 Germans, and destroyed or damaged 250 factories and 18,400 homes.

After the raid on Cologne, Arthur Harris accelerated his efforts to improve Bomber Command: radar became more sophisticated, so it could pick up features

AIR DEFENSE

As the Allied air campaign intensified, the Germans improved their air defenses. They used radar to direct searchlights and antiaircraft guns, also known as flak. A line of searchlights and guns was established along the German border to shoot down bombers before they reached their targets. Luftwaffe fighters also used radar to locate enemy bombers in the campaign to protect German cities.

The U.S. Army Air Force Arrives

With the entry of the United States into the war in December 1941, the bombing offensive against Germany expanded. On July 1, 1942, the first United States Army Air Force (USAAF) B-17 Flying Fortress bombers arrived in Britain. By mid-August the USAAF Eighth Air Force had three bomber groups in Britain with more than 100 aircraft. The B-17s were new, heavy, four-engine, high-altitude bombers that would play a vital role in the air attacks on Germany. The USAAF commanders preferred precise daytime tactical bombing to area bombing. The B-17 plus a new optical aid named the Norden sight allowed them to achieve a high degree of accuracy.

such as river estuaries and cities. Harris formed Pathfinder units, which dropped flares in order to illuminate targets before the main bomber force arrived. He also further increased the numbers of bombers in production. By the end of 1942, more than 260 four-engine bombers were attacking Germany every night with ever-increasing accuracy. Harris's aim was to increase his force to 6,000 bombers.

→ This photograph shows the result of U.S. bombing of shipyards at Kiel, Germany, in May 1943.

← German soldiers operate an 88mm antiaircraft gun in March 1941.

including the Dambusters Raid of May 16, when the RAF used newly invented bouncing bombs to destroy key dams in the Ruhr.

Bombing of Hamburg

In an operation codenamed Gomorrah, for the Biblical city that was destroyed by fire because of its wickedness, Harris planned to bomb the historic city and port of Hamburg on the Elbe River in north Germany. On the night of July 24, 733 RAF bombers attacked Hamburg. They were protected by a new device called Window that jammed the German radar defenses. Next day, USAAF bombers continued the attack. The Allied raids lasted until August 2, dropping 9,000 tons of bombs on the city. The raids devastated Hamburg. The old wooden roofs caught fire and strong winds fanned the flames to create firestorms that engulfed buildings, sucking in waves of air that pulled people into the inferno. By the end of the raids, the center of the city was a smoldering ruin. About 45,000 German civilians had died—about 10

For spring 1943, the British and Americans planned Operation Pointblank. This was a coordinated campaign against 58 German towns and cities to target the aircraft, submarine, oil, transportation, and armaments industries. The RAF would bomb at night and the USAAF during the day. The Americans still lacked men in Britain and so the majority of the bombing fell to the British. Harris's first target was the German industrial Ruhr region including the city of Essen, on which he planned a four-month offensive. Around 18,500 raids took place in the region before July 1943,

ARTHUR "BOMBER" HARRIS

British Air Chief Marshal Arthur Harris was in charge of Bomber Command from early 1942. He believed that area bombing was far more effective than precision bombing. Many senior air commanders disagreed, however. The high civilian casualties caused by Allied raids in Germany were controversial even during the war.

⬆ Incendiary bombs dropped by U.S. bombers fall on the German city of Hamburg on July 26, 1943.

percent of the German civilian total for the whole war. The Germans were anxious that more similar attacks would damage national morale, but in fact the Allies did not yet have the resources to launch further offensives on such a large scale.

Heavy Bombers

By July 1943, the USAAF in Britain comprised more than 600 aircraft, including long-range B-24 Liberators. The USAAF commanders wanted to use their heavy bombers, the B-17s, to attack industrial targets deep inside Germany, far beyond the range of fighter jets. They believed that the B-17s could operate without fighter protection. Each bomber had 11 heavy machine guns to defend it from enemy aircraft. Attacks on factories in the cities of Schweinfurt and Regensburg in southern Germany in August 1943 proved the commanders wrong, however. German fighters shot down 137 bombers.

Reorganization

Early in 1944, the USAAF reorganized and strengthened its forces in Britain and Italy. The U.S. Eighth Air Force in Britain and the U.S. Fifteenth Air Force, which was based in Italy, now had more than 1,000 heavy bombers between them. Losses were still heavy, however, the USAAF losing an average of 10 percent of the aircraft taking part in any raid.

The arrival of the new P-51 Mustang fighters changed this. These aircraft carried external, disposable fuel tanks and could provide fighter cover for raids

deep inside Germany. The Mustang had a huge impact on the air war—it made Allied bombing raids far more effective and destroyed large numbers of Luftwaffe fighters.

"Big Week"

The USAAF intensified its bombing campaign in what became known as "Big Week." On February 20, 1944, the

➜ A German 105mm antiaircraft gun could fire 15 rounds per minute.

FLYING FORTRESS

The Boeing B-17 Flying Fortress was one of the most famous aircraft of World War II. It was first developed in 1938 as a high-altitude, long-distance, heavily armed heavy bomber. More than 12,500 were manufactured. They were used mainly in Europe, though also in the Pacific theater. The aircraft became renowned for their ability to keep flying even after they sustained heavy damage.

U.S. Eighth Air Force launched the largest aerial attack of the war to date. Some 941 bombers and 700 fighters attacked aircraft factories in central Germany with the loss of just 21 bombers. That night the RAF continued the attack with a 600-bomber raid on Stuttgart, another center of German aircraft production.

The following raids were not to prove as successful. When the Eighth Air Force resumed its attack two days later, heavy fog in England caused several bombers to collide. German fighters surprised the U.S. pilots as they crossed into Germany, shooting down 44 of the 99 bombers before they reached their targets.

The U.S. Fifteenth Air Force flew from Italy and had more success. Both the British and the Americans resumed their attacks on February 24, with major raids. Big Week ended with another day of heavy bombing on February 25. This time the two U.S. air forces converged on Messerschmitt aircraft factories at Regensburg and Augsburg in southern Germany, devastating their targets.

Bombing Berlin

Arthur Harris believed that destroying Berlin would hasten the defeat of Germany. He had initiated a major RAF campaign of nighttime raids on the German capital beginning in November 1943. In 1944 U.S. bombers joined in, launching three huge daytime raids.

↑ A Boeing B-17 Flying Fortress bombs German positions in Italy during the Allied invasion of 1943.

← An RAF Halifax bomber flies over the German Ruhr industrial region during a daytime attack on Eickel in November 1944.

German morale was not broken. The Germans continued to upgrade their armaments production and to rebuild their destroyed factories. The air war did put a huge strain on the German war effort, however. Hitler was forced to recall 60,000 men from the Soviet Union to man air defenses in Germany, while the Luftwaffe lost many irreplaceable pilots.

The Allies planned a new campaign to prepare for the D-Day landings of June 1944. They bombed German military positions and transportation networks ahead of the landings in Normandy.

Once the landings had taken place, the focus switched. Raids on German cities continued. They included a devastating attack that destroyed Dresden in February 1945. Up to 25,000 civilians died after the incendiary bombs caused a firestorm. Allied bombers also supported ground forces as they fought their way across northern Europe to the Rhine River and into Germany itself.

SCIENCE AND TECHNOLOGY

World War II saw some of the most influential technological advances of the 20th century as scientists tried to give their nations the military advantage.

Scientists in the Axis and Allied countries played a key role in the war effort. Politicians and military leaders hoped to gain an advantage on the battlefield or in the air by having better weapons than the enemy, or they looked for improvements that would make industrial processes more efficient. Although many of the advantages in technology had short-term goals, their effects lasted long after the war.

Rockets and Explosives

Discoveries in physics and chemistry revolutionized bombs, missiles, and rockets. The improved weapons helped overcome the advantage tanks had gained in land battles in the first years of the war. Before World War II, most explosives were based on chemicals that had been in use since the 1860s. They gave off a bright light that revealed an artillery or naval position to the enemy

↓ Amphibious DUKWs carry supplies across a beach after landing in France on D-Day, June 6, 1944.

← Allied soldiers prepare
to fire a bazooka at a German
armored vehicle in France.

at night. New explosives developed in
World War II used different chemicals
that exploded at lower temperatures and
made no flash.

New Generation of Missiles

Being able to attack without being seen
was a great advantage. So, too, was
being able to hit targets more accurately.
The U.S. rocket scientist Robert Goddard
had built a practical missile as early as
1918. Early in World War II, Goddard's
former assistant, Clarence Hickman,

ICE SHIPS

One of the strangest
scientific ideas of the war
was an Allied plan to make
ships from icebergs. The
huge vessels would be made
from ice mixed with wood
pulp, which made it about
100 times stronger. Ships
would be strong enough to
carry aircraft and could
not be broken apart by
bombs. A refrigerator
plant would prevent them
from melting. Although
test versions were built,
no ice ship was produced
during the war.

KEY THEMES

helped to develop the bazooka, a hand-launched rocket designed as an antitank weapon. It was fired from a tube at shoulder level and had a range of up to 600 feet (182 m). It became one of the most widely used weapons of the war. U.S. forces fired around 15 million bazooka rockets during the war.

Missiles themselves also became more deadly. In the late 1880s a U.S. chemist named Charles E. Munroe had learned that missiles were more powerful if they

were topped with a hollow cone of explosive wrapped around a metal core. The open end of the cone faces the target. When the missile detonates, it creates a high-speed jet of gas and molten metal. The jet shoots forward at speeds of 19,000 miles per hour (31,000 km/h). The new missiles could penetrate one-foot-thick (30-cm) tank armor.

Sea Warfare

Technological development was extremely important in the war at sea, particularly in relation to submarines. At the start of the war, submarines had diesel engines that used oxygen to burn their fuel. That system worked well on the surface, but underwater there was not enough

⬇ A Russian T-34 tank crosses a river. Its snorkel air tube allowed it to become completely submerged.

oxygen to power diesel batteries, so submarines had electric batteries. The batteries needed to be recharged on the surface, leaving the submarine vulnerable to enemy aircraft.

From 1940, German submarine designers introduced a "snorkel," or breathing tube, to supply oxygen to diesel engines underwater. Snorkels broke away easily, however, so scientists came up with a way to allow submarines to create their own oxygen from tanks of hydrogen peroxide (a compound of hydrogen and oxygen).

Amphibious Warfare

Amphibious warfare—troops landing from the sea—was vital in both the Pacific and European theaters of the war. U.S. forces carried out a series of landings on small islands in the Pacific, while in

↑ P-51 Mustangs fly over Europe. They carried external fuel tanks to increase their range.

OFFICE OF SCIENTIFIC RESEARCH AND DEVELOPMENT

In June 1941 President Franklin D. Roosevelt created the Office of Scientific Research and Development (OSRD). Its task was to improve U.S. weapons, from bombs to small arms; to improve detection devices such as radar; and to improve the medical care of U.S. military personnel. The scientists who worked for OSRD had access to generous funds, which they used to make a whole series of scientific breakthroughs.

KEY THEMES

Europe the landings in northern France on D-Day, June 6, 1944, formed the largest amphibious operation in history.

President Franklin D. Roosevelt set up the U.S. Office of Scientific Research and Development (OSRD) in 1941. It was given the task of building amphibious military vehicles that could operate equally well on land or at sea. OSRD scientists working with General Motors Corporation invented a DUKW (known as a "duck"). The DUKW was a large boat body on top of a truck chassis with buoyancy tanks to help it float, wheels for land use, and a propeller for use at sea. U.S. factories produced some 21,000 DUKWs during World War II.

War in the Skies

Airplane developments were key to the war effort. At their heart were aerodynamics, the study of how air travels around moving objects. Engineers tried to reduce air resistance in order to allow fighters to fly faster and higher and bombers to carry bigger loads and fly farther. U.S. Engineers of the National Advisory Committee on Aeronautics (a forerunner of the National Aeronautics and Space Administration, or NASA)

designed the P-51 Mustang fighter in 1940. Its areodynamic wing and body design gave it a top speed of around 440 miles per hour (700 km/h) and a range of around 950 miles (1,530 km).

In 1939, Russian-born U.S. engineer Igor Sikorsky developed the world's first working helicopter. It used a spinning rotor with several blades to generate lift (upward force) to keep it in the air. The helicopter had two advantages over an airplane: it did not need a runway and it could hover in mid-air. The Allies used several helicopters in the Pacific to fly rescue and medical missions.

→ The Sikorsky VS-300 first flew in 1940. Although used by the Allies in the Pacific, helicopters had little impact on the war.

← This photo taken from a London roof shows a V-1 flying bomb falling on the city.

The Jet Engine

One technological development that had little effect during World War II but which had a huge effect later was the jet engine. A jet engine generates power by burning fuel and air in an enclosed space, and then throwing a jet of hot gas out as exhaust. British engineer Frank Whittle built the first jet engine in 1937 but two years later it was a German engineer, Hans Pabst von Ohain, who created the first operational jet airplane, the Heinkel He 178.

WERNHER VON BRAUN

The German scientist Wernher von Braun led the development of rocket science in the 1930s and 1940s. He designed the V-2 flying bomb, which was first launched in September 1944. After the German surrender, Von Braun and his team were taken to the United States. Their research formed the basis of the U.S. space program. Von Braun became a U.S. citizen in 1955.

KEY PEOPLE

By the middle of 1944, both Germany and Britain had jet fighters: the Germans had Messerschmitt Me 262 and the British had the Gloster Meteor, but jets generally arrived too late to have any major impact on the war.

Rocket Science

Germany led the way in rocket-launched missiles. Their leading rocket scientist Wernher von Braun (1912–1977) developed two long-range weapons, named V-1 and V-2. With a range of up to 150 miles (240 km), the V-1 was a self-propelled bomb that steered itself using onboard compasses. Its engine was designed to cut out so that it would fall and explode when it hit the ground. It was hard to aim acurately.

In late 1944, the V-2 was introduced. It was more accurate and quicker than the V-1. The Germans aimed it mainly at targets in France, Belgium, and England.

The Atom Bomb

The most important development in weaponry was the atom bomb. In the middle of 1942, President Roosevelt created a $2 billion project to build a U.S. atomic bomb. The program was code-named the "Manhattan Project" and it

occupied leading Allied physicists for most of the war. They had to figure out how to release the huge energy that could be generated by splitting atoms.

On July 16, 1945, the United States successfully tested the first atomic bomb at the Alamogordo Air Base in New Mexico. Weeks later, U.S. bombers dropped atomic bombs on the Japanese cities of Hiroshima and Nagasaki.

➔ A Japanese American soldier talks on a portable radio set during U.S. Army maneuvers.

← A member of the British Women's Auxiliary Air Force tracks German aircraft by radar.

Information War

As well as military advances, World War II brought about changes in the way that wars would be fought in the future by improving how information is gathered. One of the biggest changes came with the invention of a radio-based detection system called radar. Radar transmitters could be set up on the ground or fitted to ships or aircraft. They beamed out high-frequency radio waves; when the waves hit an object (such as an aircraft), they bounced back. By timing how long it took for the reflected beam to return, radar equipment could precisely locate objects, even if they were moving.

Robert Watson-Watt, a British scientist, introduced the first radar system in 1935. By the start of the war, the British had set

ATOMIC SCIENCE

An atom is the smallest piece of an element that can exist, but atoms are made up of particles called protons, neutrons, and electrons. They are held together by energy. In late 1942 the Italian physicist Enrico Fermi showed that splitting an atom of uranium released this energy and started a chain reaction that split more atoms, creating a huge explosion. Fermi's work was a key part of the Manhattan Project.

KEY WEAPONS

↑ This French warship is painted in experimental camouflage to disguise it at sea by breaking up its outline.

J. ROBERT OPPENHEIMER

J. Robert Oppenheimer was a theoretical physicist who was selected to lead the Manhattan Project. He had a special secret laboratory built at Los Alamos, New Mexico, where he gathered the Allies' leading physicists. His team successfully tested the first atom bomb nearby on July 16, 1945.

up radar stations along the south coast of England to detect enemy aircraft. Radar was also used in a new missile detonator. First used in 1943, a proximity fuse in the nose of a missile exploded the weapon just before it hit its target, which greatly increased its effectiveness.

The British Prime Minister Winston Churchill saw such inventions as part of what he called the "wizard war." Another element of the "wizard war" was Colossus, the world's first programmable digital computer. It was built by British scientists for codebreakers at Bletchley Park, England, who used it to help crack secret German military codes.

The war spurred on development in areas such as materials and medicine. The need for lighter airplanes, stronger tanks, and more effective missiles drove the development of plastics and alloys (mixtures of metals).

Fewer lives were lost to disease with the discovery of antibiotics such as penicillin, which stopped battlefield wounds from becoming infected. The introduction of the chemical spray DDT from 1939 reduced the number of disease-carrying insects (although it was later found to be harmful to people and the environment).

Allied Victory

The Allied use of scientific research played a major part in their victory. Radar helped to stop the Germans from gaining air supremacy during the Battle of Britain in 1940. The bazooka helped Allied forces regain North Africa from the Germans in 1942. Amphibious vehicles, such as the DUKW, played a vital role in the D-Day landings and in many assaults on Pacific islands. The Germans also had scientific victories, particularly in rocket technology, but it was Allied science that ended the war in 1945 when the atom bomb was dropped on Hiroshima and Nagasaki in Japan. However, the shadow of the atom bomb was to hang over the world for decades to come.

➔ A mushroom cloud rises from the atomic bomb dropped on the Japanese city of Hiroshima on August 6, 1945.

ESPIONAGE AND CODEBREAKING

During wartime, nations used any means they could to gather useful information about the enemy. One way was spying. Another was breaking enemy codes.

I PLEDGE ALLEGIANCE

and

SILENCE ABOUT THE WAR

WPA WAR SERVICES of LA.

Spying was a vital part of war. Knowing what the enemy was planning was an advantage. But espionage was often dangerous. Secret services recruited agents in enemy countries, or sent them in secretly. There was also espionage activity in neutral countries, such as Spain, where people from combatant countries mingled freely. No one ever knew what information might prove useful to the enemy.

German Intelligence

When the war started Wilhelm Canaris, then the head of the German military intelligence service (the Abwehr), already had his agents in place. His 30-strong spy ring, based in the United States, collected

← Posters reminded American civilians not to discuss anything that might help spies.

a careless word...

A NEEDLESS LOSS

← Government propaganda
warned their citizens
that any breach of
security could be fatal.

(SOE) and the U.S. Office of Strategic Services (OSS) were the equivalent of the Abwehr. The SOE, set up in 1940, sent hundreds of agents into Europe. Their job was to carry out sabotage in enemy territory, such as destroying railroad lines and blowing up factories, and to coordinate propaganda. One of the key requirements for SOE agents was fluency in a foreign language. Many of the agents were women. They blended in well with

and photographed useful information. The spies sent the information back to Germany in tiny microdots only 0.04 inches (1 mm) across. Canaris's other agents worked in a range of different jobs. They included a cement-factory worker in France, who obtained plans of French fortifications.

Secret Services

Both the British and the Americans set up organizations to coordinate Allied agents. Britain's Special Operations Executive

GERMAN SPIES IN AMERICA

German attempts to spy in the United States largely ended in May 1942. Eight German agents were arrested soon after they landed in the United States. Six were executed and the other five were imprisoned. Another agent was arrested in Canada. He had aroused suspicion by carrying a matchbox from a bar in Belgium, a country occupied by the Germans.

KEY THEMES

the local community. Women also had a reputation for being able to deal with stress better than men.

The OSS and SOE

The U.S. and British spy organizations both worked with resistance movements in occupied countries. The SOE worked with the French Resistance and played a vital role in preparing for the D-Day landings of June 6, 1944. It supplied more than 500,000 weapons to the French Resistance and flew more than 800 missions to France between 1941 and 1944. The SOE used special aircraft, which could land on fields at night.

The OSS meanwhile carried out espionage and sabotage missions. It trained Yugoslavian partisans to fight the Germans and trained Germans refugees to spy inside Germany. It also helped train guerrillas in Southeast Asia who fought alongside American forces in the Pacific.

Codes and Codebreaking

In addition to spying, another key to gaining information about the enemy was to intercept communications. Security was vitally important. On the home fronts, people were warned not to give away any information through careless chatter. Closer to the front, both sides sought ways to keep their long-distance radio communications secret. They used codes and ciphers (a code is a series of symbols or signs with hidden meanings; a cipher is a type of code that substitutes individual symbols or letters). Because most radio signals could be intercepted, breaking the enemy's codes became a vital way to help win the war.

"..... but of course it mustn't go any further!"

CARELESS TALK
COSTS LIVES

← In this British cartoon, Axis officers in the overhead luggage racks listen in to a conversation on a train.

Since the 1920s, the Germans had used a complex coding machine to send military messages. The device, called Enigma, looked a little like a typewriter, but had a series of rotors beneath the keys that turned a written message into what appeared to be a random set of numbers. The settings of the rotors changed every day, so Allied codebreakers were always working on codes that were already out of date. The German Navy had the most secure codes, while the Luftwaffe codes were the least secure.

Cracking the Enigma

Cracking the Enigma code became a top priority for the Allies. They knew how it worked, because their Polish allies had

➔ German soldiers send a message on an Enigma machine. The machine's rotors generated millions of possible ciphers.

ESPIONAGE IN LATIN AMERICA

The Abwehr organized a spy network in Latin America, particularly in Argentina, Brazil, and Chile. Spies collected information on shipping movements to help German submarines find merchant ships sailing to Britain. Thanks in part to help from fascist Spain, the networks were reasonably successful. Once the United States entered the war in December 1941, however, that changed. The United States used its influence to have German agents in Brazil and Chile arrested, though those in Argentina operated until the end of the war.

KEY THEMES

ALAN TURING

The British scientist Alan Turing was one of the fathers of computer science. During the war, Turing worked for the British codebreaking department at Bletchley Park. He was in charge of the work of Hut 8, which learned to decipher German naval codes. That gave the Allies a great advantage in many engagements in the Battle of the Atlantic later in World War II.

shown them an Enigma machine shortly before the start of the war. Working in secret in Bletchley Park, a manor house north of London, England, a team of scientists, mathematicians and people who were good at crosswords and math puzzles set out to crack Enigma. They devised the first computer—named Colossus—to help decipher the codes. They were also helped by the capture of an Enigma machine and codebook from a U-boat, but the Germans introduced a new level of complication to their codes. After many false starts, the codebreakers of Bletchley Park finally succeeded in decrypting the German codes in the summer of 1943.

↑ Alan Turing oversaw the construction of the Colossus computer to help with Allied codebreaking.

Germany and Britain

The Germans had no idea that their codes had been cracked. They thought increased British knowledge of U-boat operations came from an improvement in radar. Being able to read German secret intelligence gave the Allies a great advantage during the rest of the war.

The Germans themselves had successfully broken British codes from early in the war. The British used manual codes rather than machines, which made their codes comparatively easy to break. As the British studied German codes, they realized they had to make theirs more secure. By the summer of 1943, British codes were much more complicated and harder to break.

Japanese Codes

The Japanese Purple Code used a machine called Alphabetic Typewriter 97. The U.S. Army Signals Intelligence Service

⬇ Colossus was the world's first programmable electronic computer.

(SIS) mistakenly thought the typewriter had rotors, like the Enigma machine. When they realized that it had electrical switches, like a telephone exchange, the SIS built a replica machine. This allowed them to intercept not only Japanese plans, but also German plans being reported by Japan's ambassador in Berlin.

In 1942 U.S. codebreakers cracked the Japanese naval code JN-25b. It alerted them to a planned attack on Midway Island. The U.S. fleet rushed to the island. The following Battle of Midway resulted in a U.S. victory and proved a turning point in the Pacific War.

TIMELINE OF WORLD WAR II

1939 **September:** German troops invade and overrun Poland; Britain and France declare war on Germany; the Soviet Union invades eastern Poland. The Battle of the Atlantic begins.

April: Germany invades Denmark and Norway; Allied troops land in Norway.

May: Germany invades Luxembourg, the Netherlands, Belgium, and France; Allied troops are evacuated at Dunkirk.

June: Allied troops leave Norway; Italy enters the war; France signs an armistice with Germany; Italy bombs Malta in the Mediterranean.

July: German submarines (U-boats) inflict heavy losses on Allied convoys in the Atlantic; The Battle of Britain begins.

September: Luftwaffe air raids begin the Blitz—the bombing of British cities; Italian troops advance from Libya into Egypt.

October: Italy invades Greece.

December: British troops defeat the Italians at Sidi Barrani, Egypt.

1941 **January:** Allied units capture Tobruk in Libya.

February: Rommel's Afrika Korps arrive in Tripoli.

March: The Afrika Korps drive British troops back from El Agheila.

April: Axis units invade Yugoslavia; German forces invade Greece; the Afrika Korps besiege Tobruk.

June: German troops invade the Soviet Union.

September: Germans besiege Leningrad and attack Moscow.

December: Japanese aircraft attack the U.S. Pacific Fleet at Pearl Harbor; Japanese forces invade the Philippines, Malaya, and Thailand, and defeat the British garrison in Hong Kong.

1942 **January:** Japan invades Burma; Rommel launches a new offensive in Libya; Allied troops leave Malaya.

February: Singapore surrenders to the Japanese.

April: The Bataan Peninsula in the Philippines falls to the Japanese.

May: U.S. and Japanese fleets clash at the Battle of the Coral Sea.

June: The U.S. Navy defeats the Japanese at the Battle of Midway; Rommel recaptures Tobruk.

September–October: Allied forces defeat Axis troops at El Alamein, Egypt, the first major Allied victory of the war.

November: U.S. and British troops land in Morocco and Algeria.

1943

February: The German Sixth Army surrenders at Stalingrad; the Japanese leave Guadalcanal in the Solomon Islands.

May: Axis forces in Tunisia surrender.

July: The Red Army wins the Battle of Kursk; Allied troops land on Italian island of Sicily.

August: German forces occupy Italy; the Soviets retake Kharkov.

September: Allied units begin landings on mainland Italy; Italy surrenders, prompting a German invasion of northern Italy.

November: U.S. carrier aircraft attack Rabaul in the Solomon Islands.

1944

January: The German siege of Leningrad ends.

February: U.S. forces conquer the Marshall Islands.

March: The Soviet offensive reaches the Dniester River; Allied aircraft bomb the monastery at Monte Cassino in Italy.

June: U.S. troops enter the city of Rome; D-Day–the Allied invasion of northern Europe; U.S. aircraft defeat the Japanese fleet at the Battle of the Philippine Sea.

July: Soviet tanks enter Poland.

August: Japanese troops retreat in Burma; Allied units liberate towns in France, Belgium, and the Netherlands.

October: The Japanese suffer defeat at the Battle of Leyte Gulf.

December: German troops counterattack in the Ardennes.

1945

January: The U.S. Army lands on Luzon in the Philippines; most of Poland and Czechoslovakia are liberated by the Allies.

February: U.S. troops land on Iwo Jima; Soviet troops strike west across Germany; the U.S. Army heads toward the Rhine River.

April: U.S. troops land on the island of Okinawa; Mussolini is shot by partisans; Soviet troops assault Berlin; Hitler commits suicide.

May: All active German forces surrender.

June: Japanese resistance ends in Burma and on Okinawa.

August: Atomic bombs are dropped on Hiroshima and Nagasaki; Japan surrenders.

GLOSSARY

Allies One of the two groups of combatants in the war. The main Allies were Britain, the Soviet Union, the United States, British Empire troops, and free forces from occupied nations.

amphibious Describes something that operates on land and in water.

antibiotics Medicines that prevent infection by killing microorganisms.

atomic Relating to atoms, the smallest particles of a chemical element.

Axis One of the two groups of combatants in the war. The leading Axis powers were Germany, Italy, and Japan.

Blitz The German nighttime bombing campaign against British cities from September 1940 to May 1941.

convoy A group of ships or vehicles traveling together.

espionage The act of spying or the use of spies.

fascist Someone who believes in a dictatorial, militaristic political system.

flak Antiaircraft fire.

guerrillas Members of small armed groups who fight using irregular tactics such as ambush and sabotage.

incendiary Describes something that is intended to start a fire.

jet An engine that generates power by forcing out a powerful stream of gas.

Liberty Ship A merchant ship built in the United States from prefabricated parts.

mine An explosive device that detonates when it is touched.

neutral Not taking any particular side in a dispute or war.

partisans Members of a secret armed group formed to fight against an occupying force.

propaganda Material or information that is used to make people accept a particular point of view.

protectorate A country that is controlled and protected by another.

radar (Radio Detection and Ranging) A system that bounces radio waves off objects to discover their exact location.

RAF Abbreviation for the Royal Air Force, Britain's air force.

sabotage The deliberate destruction of property to gain an advantage.

snorkel A tube to allow a swimmer or vehicle to receive air underwater.

war theaters The areas in which a war is largely fought. In World War II the main theaters were Europe, the Pacific, the Eastern Front, North Africa, and the Middle East.

FURTHER RESOURCES

Books

Graham, Ian. *You Wouldn't Want to be a World War II Pilot!* Turtleback, 2009.

Hamilton, John. *War in the Air* (World War II). Abdo Publishing Company, 2011.

Jeffrey, Gary, and Terry Riley. *Battle for the Atlantic* (Graphic Modern History: World War II). Crabtree Publishing Co., 2012.

Price, Sean. *World War II Spies* (Classified). Capstone Press, 2013.

Samuels, Charlie. *Machines and Weaponry of World War II* (Machines that Won the War). Gareth Stevens Publishing, 2013.

Throp, Claire. *Spies and Codebreakers* (Heroes of World War II). Raintree, 2015.

Vansant, Wayne. *Bombing Nazi Germany* (Zenith Graphic Histories). Zenith Press, 2013.

Websites

www.ducksters.com/history/world_war_ii/
Ducksters.com links to articles about the war.

www.historyonthenet.com/ww2/home_front.htm
History.com page of links about aspects of World War II.

www.socialstudiesforkids.com/subjects/worldwarii.htm/
Index of articles about U.S. involvement in the conflict.

http://www.pbs.org/thewar/
PBS pages on the war to support the Ken Burns' film, *The War.*

http://www.pbs.org/wgbh/amex/dday/timeline/
Timeline of the war on PBS pages from The American Experience.

INDEX